To *Mom* with LOVE

From: ______________________

______________________________

Published by Christian Art Publishers
PO Box 1599, Vereeniging, 1930, RSA


First edition 2020

Designed by Christian Art Publishers
Cover designed by Christian Art Publishers
Images used under license from Shutterstock.com



Printed in China

ISBN 978-1-4321-3155-5



20 21 22 23 24 25 26 27 28 29 – 10 9 8 7 6 5 4 3 2 1

Printed in Jiaxing, China
October 2019
Print Run: 100588

# Love notes for Mom

You are

the best

MOM

in the

world.

Mothers
bring
sunshine
into the lives of their
children.

She is clothed with Strength & DIGNITY; she can laugh at the days to come.

PROVERBS 31:25

Marvelous
Optimistic
Thoughtful
Helpful
Extraordinary
Remarkable

The *joy* of the LORD is your *strength.*

Nehemiah 8:10

She speaks
with
wisdom
& faithful
INSTRUCTION
is on her tongue.
Proverbs 31:26

A mother's

is her CHILDREN.

Thank you for *teaching* me to

in the LORD with all your HEART.

Proverbs 3:5

A mother's
HEART
is a patchwork of

is PATIENT, love is KIND.
It does not envy,
it does not boast,
it is not proud.
It ALWAYS PROTECTS,
always TRUSTS,
always HOPES,
always PERSEVERES.

1 Corinthians 13:4, 7

Family
is a
little world
CREATED
by a
MOTHER'S love.

This is
the day the
LORD has made;
let us *rejoice*
AND
be glad in it.

Psalm 118:24

I am a little PENCIL in the *hand* of a writing God who is sending a *love letter* to the world.

Mother Teresa

Mom,
THANK you
for...

Many WOMEN do noble things, but YOU SURPASS them all.

Proverbs 31:29

The mother's
HEART
is the *child's*
SCHOOLROOM.

Henry Ward Beecher

My CUP overflows with blessings.

Psalm 23:5

To the world
you are just a mother,
but to your *family*
YOU ARE THE WORLD.

You make

**the best...**

"As a
MOTHER
comforts
her child,
so will I comfort
YOU."
ISAIAH 66:13

A mother holds her CHILDREN'S hands for a while, their HEARTS *forever.*

Honor her for all
that her hands have done,
& let her WORKS
bring her praise.
PROVERBS 31:31

A *mom's*
HUG LASTS
long after
she lets go.

her husband also,
and he PRAISES her.

Proverbs 31:28

God's most precious WORK OF ART is the *warmth* AND LOVE of a mother's HEART.

The *faithful* LOVE of the LORD NEVER ENDS.

LAMENTATIONS 3:22

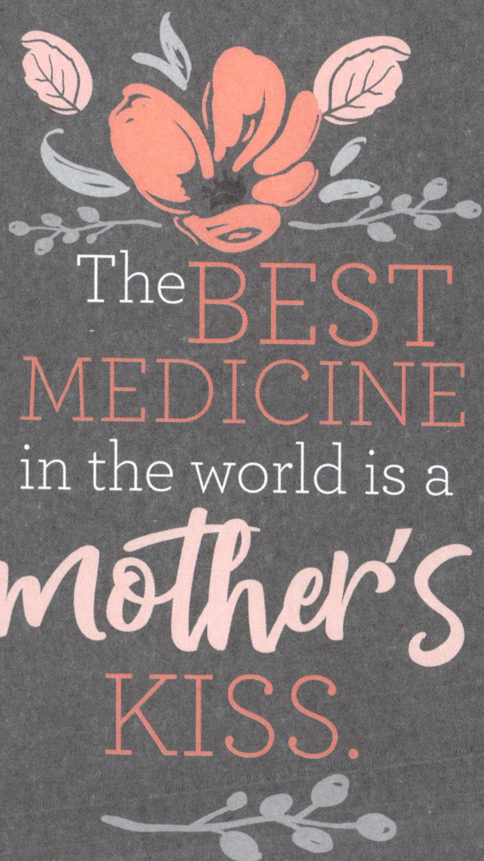
The BEST
MEDICINE
in the world is a
mother's
KISS.

LOVE
never fails.

1 Corinthians 13:8

A mother

strengthens

her children with

PRAYER,

encourages them with

HOPE and

blesses them with

LOVE.

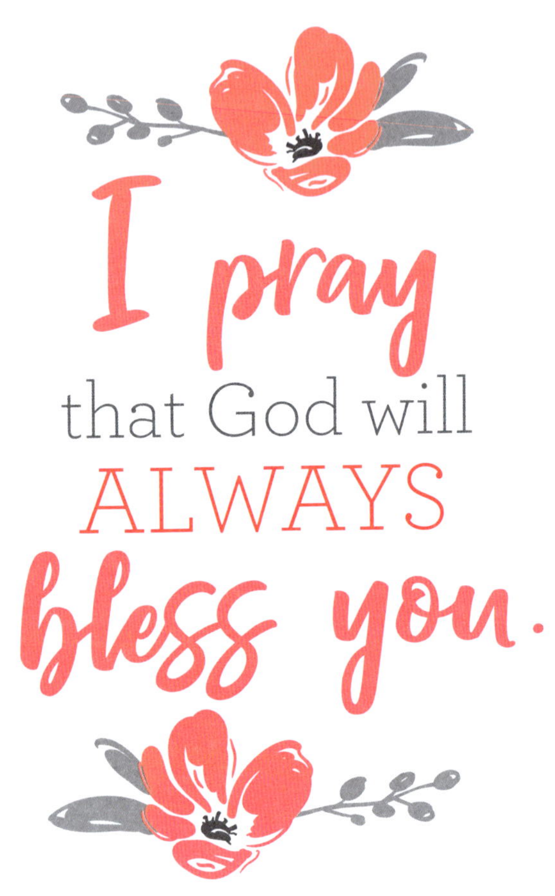
I pray
that God will
ALWAYS
bless you.

Charm is deceptive,
& BEAUTY does not last;
but a woman
who fears
THE LORD
will be
greatly praised.

PROVERBS 31:30

The best
way to spend my day
is to SPEND IT
with you!

Children are a
gift from the LORD;
they are a
REWARD
from Him.
PSALM 127:3

I love to hear *stories* about your...

A mother is the
HEART
of the
home.

The loveliest
MASTERPIECE
of the heart
of God is the
LOVE of a
mother.

Every good &
*perfect gift*
is from above,
coming down from
the Father of the
HEAVENLY
LIGHTS.

JAMES 1:17

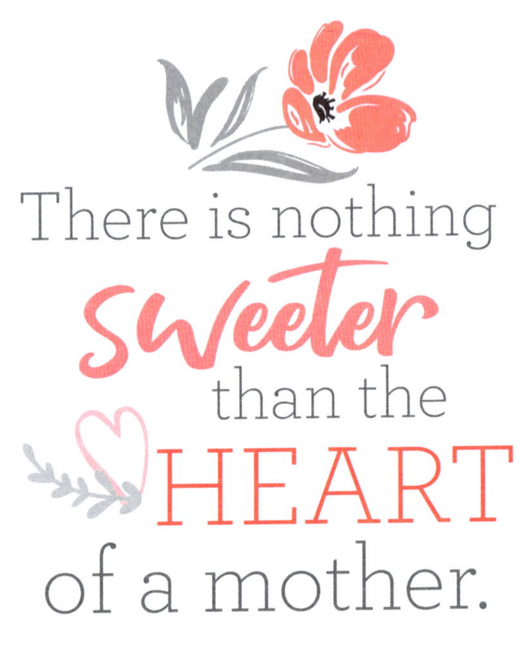
There is nothing
sweeter
than the
HEART
of a mother.

Above all
these things put on
LOVE, which is
the
bond of
PERFECTION.

COLOSSIANS 3:14

One GOOD *mother* is worth a hundred schoolmasters.

George Herbert

You are so...

By *wisdom*
a house is built,
& through understanding
it is established; through
KNOWLEDGE
its rooms are filled with
RARE &
*beautiful*
TREASURES.

PROVERBS 24:3-4

Nobody knows
of the work it makes
to keep the
HOME together,
nobody knows
of the steps it takes,
NOBODY KNOWS
*but mother.*
THANK YOU,
*Mom!*

ALL THAT I AM
or ever hope to be,
I owe to my angel
mother.

Abraham Lincoln

"GOD is with you wherever you go."

JOSHUA 1:9

Mom, I'm *grateful* for the way you...

As for me
& MY HOUSE,
we
will Serve
the LORD.
Joshua 24:15

Do small
THINGS
with
great love.

MOTHER TERESA

A
kindhearted
WOMAN
GAINS HONOR.
PROVERBS 11:16

There is more POWER IN *a mother's* HAND than in a king's scepter.

BILLY SUNDAY

A WIFE
of noble character
who can find?
She is worth far
MORE THAN

Proverbs 31:10

JOY

is the experience of knowing that you are UNCONDITIONALLY

When I was little,

I LOVED TO...

with you.

THE LORD
bless you
AND KEEP YOU.
NUMBERS 6:24

A MOTHER'S arms are made of *tenderness* and children sleep SOUNDLY in them.

Victor Hugo

"Before I formed you
in the womb
I KNEW YOU,
before you were born
I set you
APART."

JEREMIAH 1:5

Those who
HOPE
in the LORD
will renew their

Isaiah 40:31

If you have a *mom*, there is nowhere you are likely to go where A PRAYER has not already been.

Robert Brault

Never could it be POSSIBLE for any man to estimate what he owes to a godly *mother.*

CHARLES H. SPURGEON

You are the
GREATEST
Mom
EVER!

THANK YOU
for making me so
*wonderfully*
complex! Your
WORKMANSHIP
is marvelous –
how well I know it.

PSALM 139:14

A MOTHER
is your first friend,
your
best friend,
your
FOREVER friend.

The eternal GOD is your *refuge*,

& underneath are the EVERLASTING *arms*.

Deuteronomy 33:27

That SPECIAL power of LOVING that belongs to a WOMAN is seen most clearly when she becomes a

Mother Teresa

These three remain:

faith,
HOPE
& love.

But the greatest
of these is LOVE.

1 CORINTHIANS 13:13

I remember my
MOTHER'S
prayers.

They have clung to me ALL MY life.

Abraham Lincoln

You are GOD'S
masterpiece.
Ephesians 2:10

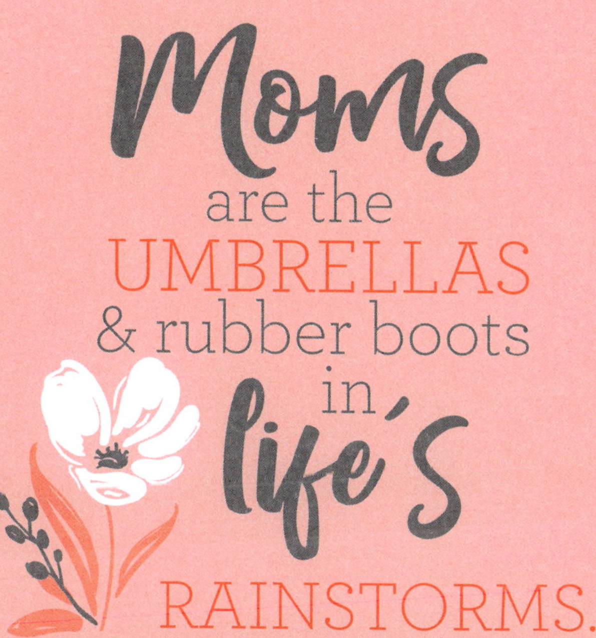
Moms
are the
UMBRELLAS
& rubber boots
in
life's
RAINSTORMS.

There is nothing in

the world

of art like

THE SONGS

mother

used to SING.

---

BILLY SUNDAY

May God grant your HEART'S *desires* and make all your PLANS *Succeed*.

Psalm 20:4

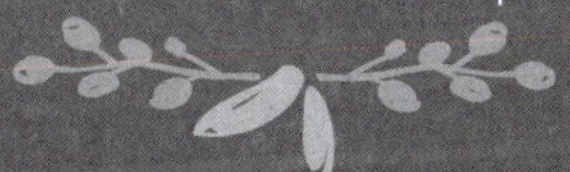

For all the
LOVING THINGS
you are & CARING
things you do,
I thank
the Lord for
GIVING ME
a special mom
LIKE YOU!

HOME
is where your
mom is.

"Where your
treasure
is, there your
HEART
will be also."

MATTHEW 6:21

We LAUGH, we cry.
We make time fly.
We are
*best friends,*
My MOTHER & I.

Nothing in all *creation* will ever be able to SEPARATE US from the

*love of God.*

ROMANS 8:39

because of you,
I am what I am today.

THANK
YOU.

Whoever dwells in the
SHELTER of the
MOST HIGH
will *rest*
in the shadow of
*the* ALMIGHTY.

PSALM 91:1

Moms
are people who
KNOW US
the BEST and
love us
THE MOST.

THANK YOU!

"Mom"
is a title above
"QUEEN."

May you be
blessed
by the LORD,
the MAKER of
heaven
& EARTH.

Psalm 115:15

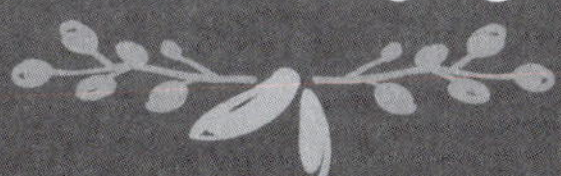

I believe

IN LOVE

at first sight
because I loved
my mom
since I opened
my eyes.

P.S.
You are
amazing
and
I LOVE YOU.